A ROCK IN GOD'S SKY

Motivational Book For Young Scholars That Combines Faith, Astronomy & Nature

Gary Anthony Tillman

RoseDog Books
585 Alpha Drive, Suite 103
Pittsburgh, PA 15238
Visit our website at *www.rosedogbookstore.com*

ISBN: 979-8-88527-921-5
eISBN: 979-8-88527-969-7

THE
AUTHOR'S PREMISE

This book is simply about the Glory of God and the author's take on astronomy from a spiritual perspective. It contains factual information but also includes faith-based opinions, and personal observations.

TABLE OF CONTENTS

The Unique Unknown

According to various research, the universe began with an enigmatic explosion in outer space over 13 billion years ago. The aftermath of this cosmic eruption led to the formation of several stars, planets, and numerous galaxies.

A few billion years after the universe was created, the solar system was established. The Sun is the center of the solar system and it was the first to form. Next, the Terrestrial and Jovian planets were constructed from the residual particles remaining after the Sun's creation.

There are nine planets in our solar system. Planets are formed in the sky from a combination of space rocks and solar winds. Based on this uncomplicated premise, each planet in its simplest form is nothing more than a massive rock in the sky.

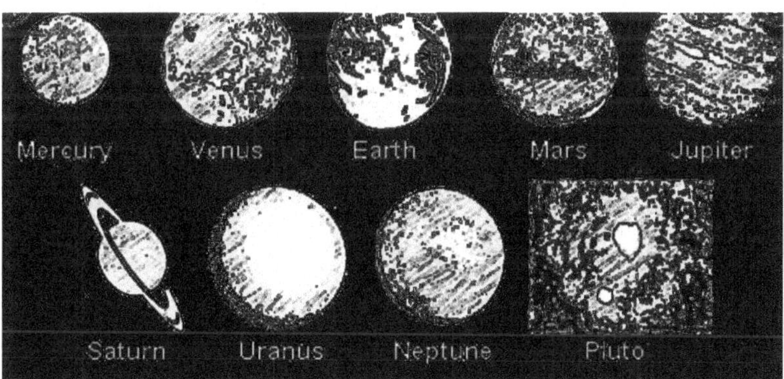

Scientists suggest that gas and dust particles from the solar system were pulled together by gravity in order to form the Earth. Therefore at its core, the foundation of the Earth's surface is made up of rock and water. In addition, the Earth has a distinctive atmosphere unlike any other planet.

Although there are numerous different accounts on the start of the Universe, the most widely accepted explanation is the Big Bang Theory. While I'm not sure if that theory is absolute, what I do know for certain is what we see was not formed by the hands of a man.

Only a spirit of Infinite Intelligence could create a World so wonderful, an Earth so enormous, and an Universe so unique…Imagine how gracious and glorious the spirit of God must be. God is so rich in his grace that he gave us life and an entire planet to inhabit as our home.

Hebrews 11:3 NKJV. *By faith we understand that the worlds were framed by the word of God, so that the things which are seen were not made of things which are visible.*

We know that life exists on Earth but there are many ambiguous components about outer space that remain a mystery. There are other galaxies that exist beyond our eyesight and technology. The Universe is significantly larger than what we can see.

From our viewpoint we see the sun, the moon, and the countless stars in the sky, but imagine from God's multilevel viewpoint. God's vision is beyond all the planets and all the various galaxies in the sky.

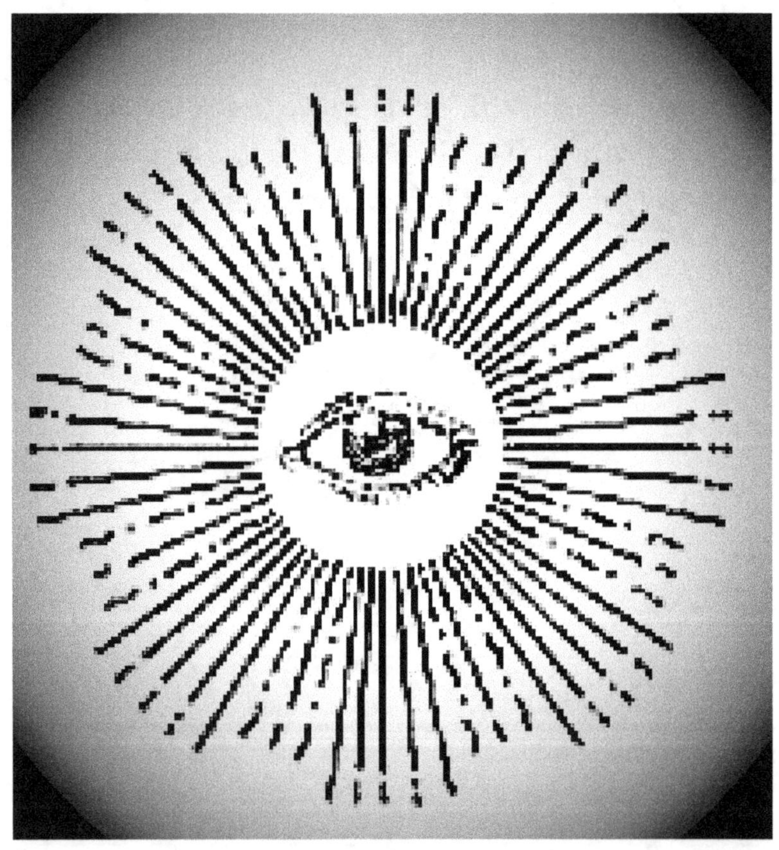

God's sovereignty is supreme. His presence reigns from the highest peak to the lowest valley.

The wisdom and the ways of God transcend any metric of measurement. His precepts are permanent and his epilogue is eternal. The spirit of God is BEYOND our imagination.

The concept "A Rock in God's Sky" is literally making it plain how colossal and clairvoyant the power of our God is. Just as humans draw on a piece of paper, the sky is God's canvas. Life and creation are God's artwork and master piece. The Earth which seems so big to You and I, is nothing more than a Rock in God's Great Sky.

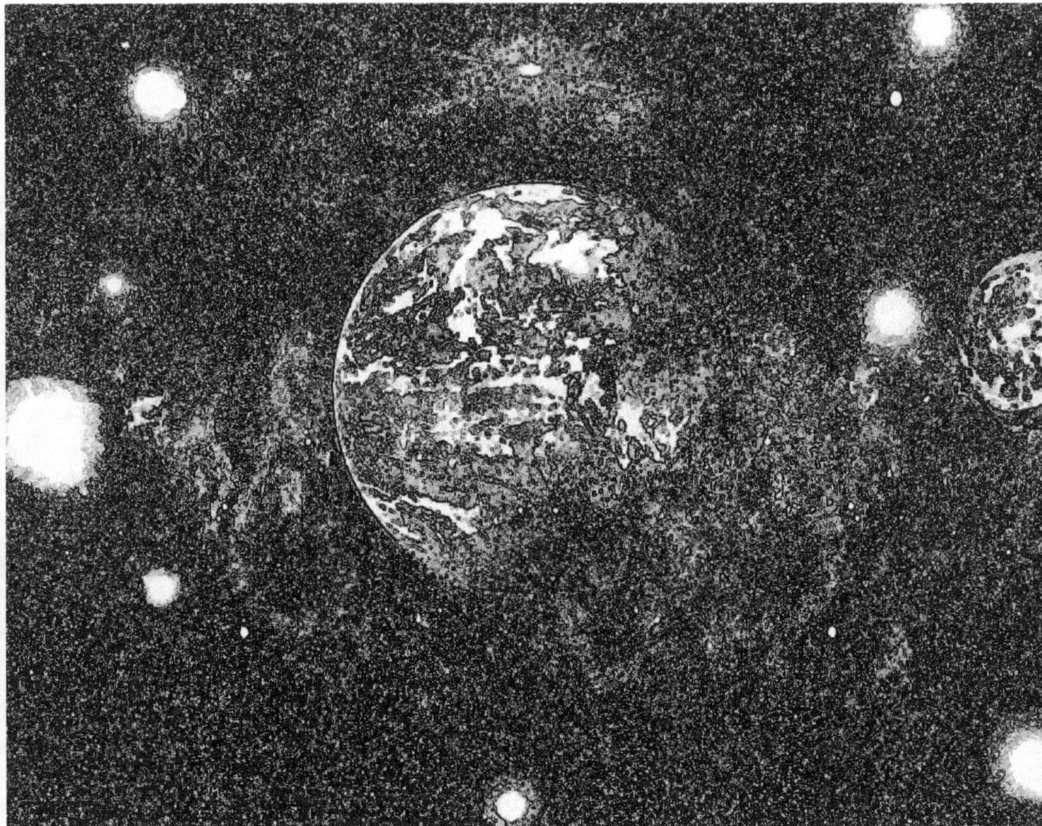

BEYOND

Original Poem By The Author

PRAISE GOD, Life is Free
But there's so much *more to see*

We are who we are
But there's so much *more to be*

We learn what we learn
But there's so much *more to know*

You weren't made to stay the same
But You were *born to grow*

THE SUN AND THE SON

One of the most beautiful sights to witness is the sunrise over the ocean blue water.

To see the rising of the sun is to see the power of God.

The sun is the star at the center of the solar system and it is the most important source for life and energy on Earth. The sun is a hot boiling ball of plasma comprised mostly of hydrogen and helium.

The temperature of the sun at its outer surface is about 10,000 degrees Fahrenheit but towards the innermost center it can get as hot as 27 million degrees. The energy and light that emanate from the sun is essential. Without the sun, life on Earth could not exist.

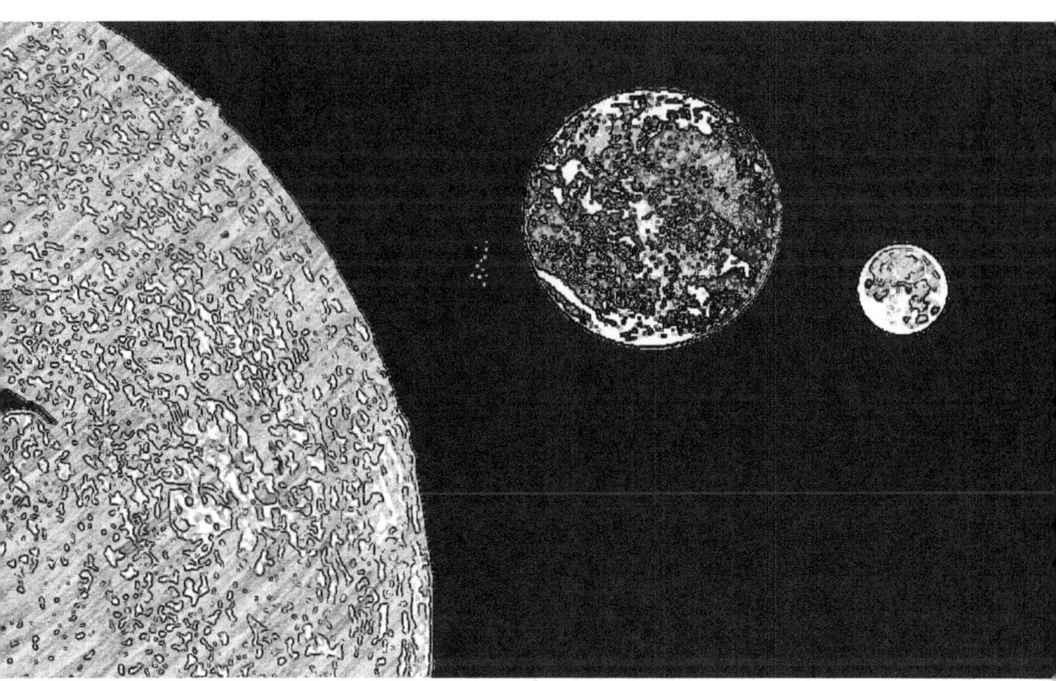

The sun gives us a glimpse of God's power and potency. With each sunrise and every sunset, another day passes.

The sky is God's playground. The Sun is his Glory. It is a privilege to witness the magnificent and majestic magic behind God's mystifying methods. The sun and nature are both synonymous with God's genius and beauty.

There are many benefits and blessings that are associated with the sun. Obviously the sun provides heat and light for the Earth , but there are additional health benefits that are associated   with the sun as well.

According to medical analysis, the sun is believed to assist the body in generating the production of vitamin D. Sunlight is also proficient in supporting bone health, lowering blood pressure, and research suggests exposure to the sun is advantageous for good mental health.

There are currently over 7 billion people in the world and every single person relies on the sun for life. It's not just humans but every living organism depends on the sun. From the birds in the sky, to the mammals on the land, to the animals in the sea.

Similar to how all living creature's rely on the same sun, we are also made from and rely on the same GOD. For those that don't believe in God, look no further than the sun for the metaphor. The sun is confirmation of God's strength, steadiness, and everlasting power. The sun gives energy to all life.

For those who are Christians and believe in Jesus Christ, we recognize him as Lord and the *son* of God. Faith teaches us that Jesus Christ is simply God's word and spirit coming down to Earth in the manifestation of a man.

Therefore Christ, the **SON** is God's power translated in the form of flesh. In a much different vein, the *SUN* is God's power in the form of nature.

FUN FACT:

Many scientists and researchers have confirmed that exposure to the sun can lead to an increase in serotonin levels. Serotonin is good because it can lead to a boost in hormones and brain stimulation. According to research, serotonin is the key hormone that stabilizes our mood, feelings of well-being, and happiness. This hormone impacts your entire body and it acts as a neurotransmitter between different cells.

The sun contains all kinds of hidden treasures. My suggestion is to get out of the confines of the house and spend more time outside with the Sun. God created it for us all to enjoy!

CHAPTER 3:

MIDNIGHT MOONLIGHT

The moon is most popularly known as the Earth's natural satellite because it orbits and travels around the Earth. It takes approximately anywhere from 27 to 29 days for the moon to complete one full orbit.

As the Earth rotates around the sun, the moon orbits around the Earth. This is the main reason why the moon was historically used by scientists to calculate time. The moon is the Earth's only orbiter.

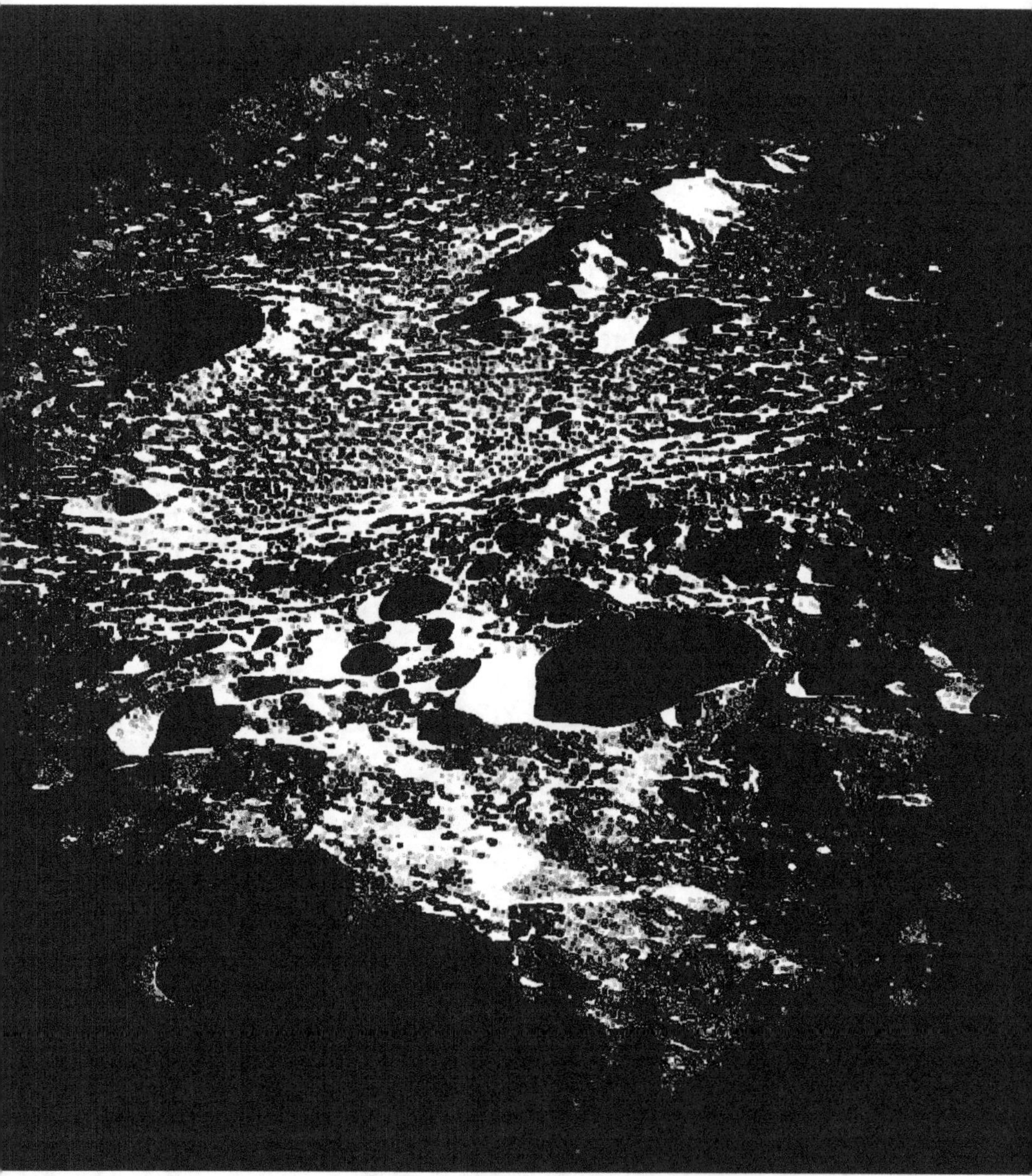

Space rocks, asteroids, and meteors from outer space collide with the moon and cause craters. These craters remain visible because there is no erosion on the moon. The moon has no atmosphere, weather, wind, or water; therefore it doesn't have the same natural elements that the Earth possesses. The moon contains no life.

Another attribute about the moon is that it is extremely dark. Consequently when we see moonlight that's actually the light from the sun reflecting off the moon . The sun is so bright that it provides light for the moon even when it's hidden from view.

The illumination from the Sun on the Moon provides a beautiful image in the night sky.

The moon is not a planet or a star. From the Earth's vantage point, the moon clearly looks like a rock in God's sky. The funny thing about it is the same way we look and see the moon in the sky. That is the same way the Earth would look if we were standing on the moon. The Earth is rotating on its axis but it is also levitated in the sky.

The difference is while the moon's image is dormant and gray, the Earth's appearance in the sky is a beautiful blue-speck full of life. Although the Moon and the Earth are humongous in comparison to humans, they are nothing more than a rock in God's Sky.

Early scientists used the moon's posture and position in the sky to help determine time. The calendar that we use today was heavily influenced by the observation of the moon's rotation.

The moon's effect on the Earth can't be understated. The gravitational pull by the Moon and Sun are responsible for high and low tidal waves in the Earth's ocean waters.

FUN FACT:

There was a recent real life example where the presence and the pull of the moon's gravity showed its relevance to the Earth's ocean and seawaters. In March of 2021, there was a logjam in the Suez Canal in Egypt. The Suez Canal is an ancient man-made water pathway that connects the Mediterranean Sea and The Red Sea for the import and export of goods. A logjam is when something is stuck in a water pathway or a river.

In this specific case, there was a ship containing goods, toiletries, and supplies that got jammed in the narrow pathway of the Suez Canal river. The ship was stuck for almost a full week. Not only did the ship block the river, but it also stopped other ships from traveling therefore causing a delay of many supplies and services to various communities.

However, according to *The Guardian* and *CNN.com,* as well as other credible sources, the full moon at the end of March 2021 provided a high spring tide among the Earth's seawaters. As a result, this high tide gave the ship the breathing room it needed and assisted in dislodging the ship from being stuck.

This example illustrates the direct connection between The Earth and The Moon.

CHAPTER 4

WHAT'S UP

In astronomy the sky is often referred to as the "sky bowl" or the celestial sphere. In basic terms, the sky is defined as anything above the ground of the Earth. In the sky we get a reminder of God's peace through the beautiful clouds, the light of the sun , and the moon. In that same sky we also get an indication of God's wrath and his Almighty Power.

From the sky we see the eccentric electric charge of lightening. We hear the riveting rambunctious roar of thunder. In contrast, when the storm is over, we see the remarkable refulgence of God's beauty through radiant rainbows. The sky is full of many wonders.

The collage of clouds in the sky are a beautiful sight to observe. Clouds consist of a combination of water particles and ice crystals. Whether it's snow, hail, or rain, each is formed in the various celestial conditions within the cloud.

Clouds are important to the atmosphere and they play a huge role in regulating the energy and weather.

Hoe gaat het?(Dutch)
Quoi de neuf.(French)
Que pasa.(Spanish)

Or in America better wise know as "What's Up". This phrase was once used as slang but it has spread and become a general greeting throughout most of the world

Obviously the question is not to be taken literally. Nonetheless it's ironic that people all over the world say what's up but most people rarely take the time to actually look up at the sky.

To observe the beautiful blue sky that God made to cover and keep us. To look at the tree line that provides an illustrious image of God's artistry. The most harmonious things in life are free.

Everyone is in a hurry. Just like myself, people are so busy looking at directly what's in front of them, from their television, to their phones, to their problems. We don't take time to pause and honor this beautiful Earth God created for us.

Everyone is so bogged down with the worries and concerns of life, we forget that God has it all covered. There are many trials and tribulations in life but there is so much more to rejoice over. Choose beauty over ashes.

This book is a friendly reminder to take a pause to absorb the complex captivating qualities of God, the universe, and nature.

Moment

Original Poem By The Author

Take a moment and look at the *trees*
Hear the singing of the birds
The buzzing of the *bees*

Take a moment and gaze in the *clouds*
See the great blue sky
And the sun shining *proud*

Take time to refine your mind
Find the peace within your *soul*
No need to worry or hurry
God has it ALL under *control*

CHAPTER 5:

UNIVERSE (U-N-I VERSE)
Law Of Attraction

The universe is the basic compilation of all existence. It includes the planets, the stars, all organisms, and even the intangible things such as space and time.

The Collins dictionary defines the universe as the totality of all things that exist. However the word itself has two parts, a prefix and suffix. (UNI/VERSE)

Uni is derived from Latin language and it means one. **Verse is** defined in the Webster dictionary as writing arranged in a mythical rhythm or in lines. So altogether the word breaks down to mean one verse.

It is my personal belief that each human is in a song and dance with the universe. We get one song, one verse, or in essence one life. We were giving a producer, a beat; and it is our application of faith that determine what kind of song we make.

Therefore since our actions and attitude play a key role in the results in our life, it is my personal opinion that every human is in an interactive relationship with the universe.

This theory is similar to the old science colloquialism, *Like Attracts Like.* According to science, *the thoughts and energy that we project into the world is likely to be what we attract in our own personal lives.* So consequently by our thoughts and actions we hold the keys to our dreams, desires, and destiny.

Humans are made in the image of God and according to the bible, we are to imitate GOD.

CREATE, CARE, AND SHARE

Ephesians 5:1 NKJV Therefore be imitators of God as dear children.

It was not a mistake or by happenstance that God created the Earth. There was no coincidence but GOD has a purpose. Each man, woman, boy, and girl regardless of race, culture, or creed were all made by GOD.

Since God doesn't make mistakes, that means every individual has potential. We all have a touch of God's spirit and greatness inside us.

The author is far from a preacher or a teacher. I am not a saint nor a scientist but this is not a sermon or a study. This is an honest observation from one of God's creations. The same GREAT GOD that created the Earth and the Universe also created me and you. And by his grace, we are all Great! Walk in Victory!!!

For God's word says:

" *HE WHO IS IN YOU IS GREATER THAN HE WHO IS IN THE WORLD* "
(1st JOHN 4:4 NKJV)

The truth of the matter is the Earth is over 4 billion years old and its circumference is nearly 25,000 miles long. What force other than God can keep this massive land of rock and water steady on its axis, while suspended in the middle of the stratosphere?

The Earth which seems so big to **You and I** is nothing more than a Rock in God's Great **Sky!**

Seasons

Original Poem By The Author

It was already written.
*It was already **done***
The battle has been fought
*And the war has been **won***

Peaks and valleys of life
*Are similar to **seasons***
A path to a journey
*And God has a **reason***

Some things are unjust
*Some things are **unfair***
But you are never alone
*For God is always **there***

In the autumn the leaves fall
*And in the spring they **grow***
So never get too high
*And never get too **low***

Don't rush to be old
*But enjoy being **young***
'Cuz life is like season
*Your time will **come***